# Music Scales

Learn about all the different types of music
scales you can use in music

3rd Edition

by

Andrew Milner

First published online by Andrew Milner in 2021

3$^{rd}$ edition published by Andrew Milner in 2025

Find me on Instagram: @andrewmilnermusic

Even more about me:
https://linktr.ee/AndrewMilner

# TABLE OF CONTENTS

# Chapter 1 – Introduction

Hello there and welcome to the beginning of this Musical Scales booklet. This is a book dedicated to those who want to learn all about musical scales, how they are built and where you can use them.

We'll start by going through the necessary music theory concepts required to understand what we're talking about here.

Afterward, we'll go through major and minor scales, which are the most common ones used in music. We will also talk about advanced scales such as chromatic scales, modal scales, blues scales, pentatonic scales, and many more concepts.

# Chapter 2 – Music theory concepts

## 2.1 Naming and notating notes

A **note** is the musical equivalent of a **letter** in a word, in that it is the base unit used to create music. There are a total of **seven** different base notes. These notes can be **altered**, thus creating new notes, by using what is known as **accidentals**, but more on that in a future chapter. Notes have many names, but the following two naming conventions are the most common:

- the first ones uses the first **seven** letters of the English alphabet: A, B, C, D, E, F, G; in some cases you may also find a **number** after the letter

- the second one uses a **Neo-Latin** set of names: La, Si, Do, Re, Mi, Fa, Sol

Throughout this series and this blog in general, I will be using the **letter** notation instead of the Neo-Latin one since I am used to is more and generally speaking other chapters you may have encountered also use this notation. And with regards to the number, it signals what **octave** the note is a part of. More on that in the next chapter.

And since a picture speaks a thousand words, here is a graphic representation of the easiest musical scale out there, the **C major** (or **Do major**) scale:

The notes of this scale are, in order, **C (Do)**, **D (Re)**, **E (Mi)**, **F (Fa)**, **G (Sol)**, **A (La)**, **B (Si)** and **C (Do)** once again.

## 2.2 Reading musical sheets

A musical sheet is the most common method musicians use to write their music. And this method is a universal one, meaning that it doesn't matter what instrument you play, you can always write your music on a musical sheet.

Musical sheets have various elements inside them, used to designate the **tempo** of the song, the **key** of the song, the **time signature** and of course the **notes** of the song (organized in what is known as **bars** or **measures**). Worth noting is that the areas in which the notes are actually written are called **staffs** and they consist of 5 horizontal lines, each having an empty space area and that notes are written on either the lines or the space area. More on that below.

Musical sheets can have multiple staffs. The example I am about to use is a sheet containing what is known as a **grand staff**, which is used to write a piano song. This type of staff actually contains two regular staffs, one for each hand. Other musical sheets can also contain multiple staffs, but most of the time each staff is dedicated to a different instrument. These types of sheets are extremely useful for conductors, who are required to follow several instruments at a time and need to know when each instrument starts and stops playing during a song. And there are of course sheets that contain a single staff, dedicated to a single instrument.

So, let's take a look at a musical sheet:

Quite a lot of stuff there. Let's break it down:

The **tempo** section is used to tell the musician how **fast** a piece is meant to be played. Now there are two ways in which you can specify tempo:

- using a **number** and a note duration, like in this example

- using an Italian **tempo word** such as **Andante**, **Allegro** etc.

In our case, the tempo is read as **quarter note equals 120** or **120 beats per minute (BPM)**. We'll discuss these in detail in a separate chapter.

Next up we have the **time signature**. As you can see, it consists of two numbers. The number at the bottom represents the **note duration** used to measure a **beat** in a measure while the number at the top represents the **number of beats** in a measure. In our case, the time signature is read as **four quarter notes**. We will learn about time signatures in more detail in a future chapter.

Up next is the **key signature**. This is used to tell the musician what **key (or scale)** the song is written and played in. In our case, it is a variant of the F minor key (scale) called **melodic F minor**. We will discuss this as well in more detail in a future chapter.

The next aspect is that of **clefs**. Clefs are important because they designate the **octaves** in which you are supposed to play the notes. On the top staff we have what is known as the **G2 clef**. It's called the G2 clef because its starting point is located on the line where the **G note** is located, which is the **second line** of the staff (hence the G2 name). More often than not though it can be referenced to as the G clef or treble clef.

Notes written on the G2 clef staff usually pertain to the **fourth octave** or higher. As you remember, the fourth octave is the one that starts with the **middle C** note and is also known as the **middle octave**. As a general rule, notes with medium and high pitches are placed on staffs with the G2 clef.

The clef on the lower staff is called the **F4 clef** for the same reasoning as above. Notes written on this type of staffs are usually the ones with lower pitches (or bass notes, if you will). Usually the notes on this clef are from the **third octave** or lower. Also, this clef can also be referenced to as simply the F clef or the bass clef.

As you can see, note placement is different for these clefs (e.g. the G note is on the second staff line for a G2 clef and on the 4th space area for an F4 clef). However, two rules are available for both. First, the **higher** the **pitch** of the note, the higher its **position** on the staff. And the second rule to remember is that each note has its very own position reserved on the staff, be it a line or a space. The only time this is not true, in a sense, is when you use **accidentals** but even then the notes are different, though based on the same one. We'll get to that when the time is right.

And finally, let's talk about **measures**. Measures are closely linked with time signatures in that you cannot have more notes in a measure/bar than the time signature allows you to. A measure is used to delimit a section of a song and it usually contains what is known as a **musical motif** (which is basically a group of notes that wants to transmit an idea, expressed by using notes instead of letters). Measures are separated by a vertical line called a **bar separator** and the end of a song (the **last** measure of the song) is designated by a special kind of marker, as you can see. The terms **bar** and **measure** can be used interchangeably.

Since this chapter in particular is more about reading notes, let's take a look at our good old friend, the C major scale, written in both the G2 clef and the F4 clef versions:

As you can see, we have notes both on the 5 lines of each staff and outside of them. This is of course allowed and we can write notes outside of the designated 5 lines by using **ledger lines** in the places where one would expect a staff line. Also worth noting is the alternation between lines and spaces. Two consecutive notes are located on a line and on a space area, or on a space area and then on a line, be it a staff line or a ledger line.

When it comes to the G2 clef, the notes on the lines are **E**, **G**, **B**, **D** and **F**, while the notes on the spaces in between are **F**, **A**, **C** and **E**.

When it comes to the F4 clef, the notes on the lines are **G**, **B**, **D**, **F** and **A**, while the notes on the spaces in between are **A**, **C**, **E** and **G**.

You may also notice that the notes have different lines. These are specific to their **duration**, meaning how long the note is played. In our particular example we have 16th notes on the G2 clef and whole notes and quarter notes on the F4 clef, which also has what is known as **rests** in the beginning. We will detail all of this in another chapter.

13

One final note is with regards to places where you see notes on different positions on a staff but on top of each other. That tells the musician that he needs to play **all** the notes at the same time.

## 2.3 Tones and semitones

A **semitone** (also known as a **half step**) is the smallest measuring unit or interval used in classical Western music. Frequency wise, it is equal to a twelfth of an octave or half a tone, hence the name a **half step**.

A **tone** (also known as a **step**) is composed of **two semitones**.

A simpler definition for a semitone is **the difference between two consecutive pitches** (which may or may not be part of the same scale, as we'll talk about in a future chapter).

On a piano, this translates to the difference in pitch between playing a white key and a black key found next to each other on the keyboard (sometimes you will have two white keys next to each other but never two black keys). On a guitar, this translates to the difference between two **consecutive** frets located on the **same string**.

So why are tones and semitones so important? We'll unravel this mystery chapter by chapter but for now, let's just say that they help us classify **music intervals**, **scales,** and **chords** (let's just say that the difference between a major chord and a minor chord is one semitone, placed at the right note so to speak).

Also, it's useful to understand these concepts when other musicians talk to each other about how a note is one semitone higher than another.

## 2.4 Accidentals and enharmonic notes

**Accidentals** are musical symbols which, when used on a note, **alter** its pitch by **one semitone** or **one tone**. There are 5 common accidentals in music. Here is what they look like:

So, what exactly do we have there? Well, let's take them one by one:

- the **sharp** (♯) accidental **raises** the pitch of a note by **one semitone**
- the **flat** (♭) accidental **lowers** the pitch of a note by **one semitone**
- the **natural** (♮) accidental **returns** a note to its **original pitch**
- the **double flat** (♭♭) accidental **lowers** the pitch of a note by **one tone** (or two semitones)
- the **double sharp** (𝄪) accidental **raises** the pitch of a note by **one tone** (or two semitones)

Now that we know what accidentals are, it's time to take a look at **enharmonic notes**. Enharmonic notes are two notes with **different notations** that have the exact **same pitch**.

Think of it like this. What note do you obtain when you sharpen a C? The answer is C♯. What note do you obtain when you flatten a D? The answer is D♭. However, when you actually play these notes on an instrument, you will realize that they are **one and the same**, pitch wise.

So why are there two notations? The answer to that question is closely linked to the **key** (or scale) the song is written in. We will get a firm grasp of keys when we talk about scales and the circle of 5ths.

## 2.5 Music intervals

A **musical interval** is the difference in pitch between 2 notes. There are two types of such intervals:

- **simple** – the ones we will be discussing in this chapter, and their name comes from the fact that they are located within the same octave

- **compound** – these ones are obtained by putting together two simple music intervals and they span two octaves

Simple music intervals consist of two components:

- a **number** which indicates how many **different** tones the interval contains

- a **quality** which gives us the level of **consonance** the interval has (no one's gonna ask you about this so don't worry)

Quality wise, an interval can be one of **perfect**, **major**, **minor**, **augmented** or **diminished**. The last two are out of scope for this series, so we'll be focusing only on the first 3.

We have a total of **8 simple music intervals** that we are going to discuss. The first one is called the **prime** and it consists of a **single note**. In terms of interval quality, a prime is **perfect**:

Next up is the **second**, which is the difference between two consecutive notes. Seconds can be either **major** or **minor**. Tone/semitone wise, a major second contains 1 tone, while a minor second contains 1 semitone. Here are some examples:

Next in line is the **third**. Similar to seconds, thirds can also be either **major** or **minor**. Major thirds contain 3 tones, each separated by the other by **1 tone**, while a minor third has its tones separated by a tone and a semitone respectively. Here are some examples:

As you can see, each and every interval is computed between two notes. The number giving us the name of the interval is based on how many pitches there are between the two notes, including them. In the case of the third, we have 3 tones: C, D and E.

The next interval is the **fourth**. Unlike seconds and thirds, fourths are **perfect**, quality wise. A perfect fourth consists of 2 tones and 1 semitone. A particularly interesting type of fourth is the **tritone** (which basically means it has 3 tones in it), which you'll undoubtedly notice when we play some examples in a bit:

Next up is the **fifth** musical interval. Similar to fourths, fifths are also **perfect** and they consist of 3 tones and a semitone. Here are some examples:

Our next interval is the **sixth**. Sixths can be either **major** (4 tones and 1 semitone) or **minor** (3 tones and 2 semitones). Here are some examples:

Our penultimate interval is the **seventh**. Sevenths can also be either **major** (5 tones and 1 semitone) or **minor** (4 tones and 2 semitones). Here are some examples:

And finally, we have the **octave**. Octaves are **perfect** and they consist of 5 tones and 2 semitones. Here is an example:

Generally speaking, when someone mentions an interval, they are most likely referring to it from a **rising** or **ascending** point of view. In other words, the two notes the musician thinks of have the trait that the first one has a **lower** pitch than the second one (e.g. C-E, F-A etc.).

We can think of intervals in a descending manner as well, with the first note having a **higher** pitch than the second one. This is why we've also learned about how many tones and semitones are in an interval. By using those numbers and lowering the pitch by the necessary number of tones and semitones, we will get a descending music interval.

So, why are intervals important? Well, for many reasons. The first one refers to **key signatures**, as we'll learn in more detail in the next chapter. The next important one refers to chords. I won't go into too much detail here, but let's just say that the main difference between a major chord and a minor chord, both formed on the same note, lies in the quality of the rising **third** formed by using the root note.

## 2.6 The circle of 5ths and key signatures

The circle of fifths is an actual diagram in the form of a circle, that helps us in forming **major scales** and their relative minor counterparts. The circle itself looks something like this:

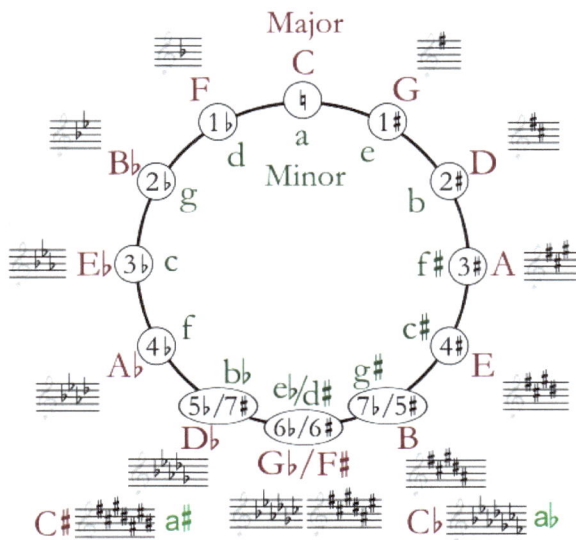

Source:
https://commons.wikimedia.org/wiki/File:Circle_of_fifths_deluxe.svg

In the image above we have all possible major scales that can be formed. Everything starts at the top with the C major scale.

So why is it called the circle of 5ths? Because the difference between each **root note** of the major scales is a **fifth**. Let's understand what this means.

If you look at the top of the diagram, as we've seen, we have the C major scale. If we go through the circle clockwise, the first major scale we encounter is the **G major** scale. The tone difference between **C** and **G** is a **rising fifth**. Next in line is the **D major scale**. The difference between G and D is once again a rising fifth and so on.

We can go through the circle counter-clockwise, the first major scale we encounter is the F major scale. The difference between C and F is of course a **falling fifth**. And so on.

One thing you may notice is that at some point these scales overlap, meaning that you have two different names for scales that seem to be one and the same. Which, enharmonically speaking, they are, because they have the same pitches, but with different names. From my experience, you will most likely **never** encounter the C♭ key (everyone will use B) or the C♯ key (everyone will use D♭). G♭ and F♯ may be used, but in the end it all boils down to preference (I usually use F♯).

Another thing to notice is that next to each scale we have a staff with a bunch of sharps or flats on it (aside from the C major scale). That, my fellow music enthusiasts, is the **key signature**.

A **key signature** refers to the **sharp notes** or **flat notes** a certain scale (or key) has. As we can see from the circle of 5ths, aside from the C major scale (and as a result A minor), every other scale has at least one accidental in their signature.

So why are key signatures important? Because when a song is written in a key that has an accidental in its signature (for example, G major), whenever you encounter the note or notes that have accidentals in the key signature (in the case of G major, it has an F♯ in its signature), then you are obligated to play those notes with the accidentals applied, **unless stated otherwise, usually by the use of a natural accidental** (in the case of G major, we will always play the F notes on the staff as F♯).

Key signatures, therefore, allow musicians to avoid placing an accidental each and every time a note should have one because of the scale it is part of. Placement wise, a key signature is located at the very beginning of a song or anywhere else a key change is required in more complex pieces of music.

# Chapter 3 – The C major and A minor scales

## 3.1 Detailing the C major and A minor scales

A **musical scale** is an ordered set of pitches that are found in the **same octave**. An octave is the frequency interval between two notes with the same fundamental pitch of which one has double the frequency of the other.

The simplest example of a major scale is the C major scale. This scale consists of the C, D, E, F, G, A and B notes. This is how it looks like:

The A minor scale consists of the A, B, C, D, E, F and G notes. Here's how it looks like:

## 3.2 Relative scales

Those of you with a keen eye will have noticed that the two scales in this chapter have the same notes but in a different order. And this observation is correct.

When it comes to music, each **major scale** has a **relative minor scale** and vice-versa. And it's pretty easy to figure out the relative of a scale.

If you want to figure out the **relative minor scale** for a **major scale**, you have to look at the **sixth note** from the **major scale**. That note will be the starting note (or **root note**) for your relative minor scale.

If you want to figure out the **relative major scale** for a **minor scale**, you have to look at the **third note** from the **minor scale**. That note will be the **root note** of the relative major scale.

In our case, the **sixth note** of the **C major scale** is **A**. As a result, the **A minor scale** will be the relative minor scale for the C major scale.

Similarly, the **third note** of the **A minor scale** is **C**. As a result, the **C major scale** will be the relative major scale for the A minor scale.

# Chapter 4 – Major and minor scales in detail

## 4.1 Major scales explained

**Major scales** contain 7 different notes, as you have seen in the previous chapter. And, as we have discussed, all these notes are located within the same octave. Each major scale begins on a note called the **root note** (or **tonic**) and ends on the same note, but an octave higher.

However, in order to have a proper major scale, notes need to be located at certain tonal distances between one another.

Let's take the C major scale as an example again. The notes are C, D, E, F, G, A, B and C, which we end the scale on. Based on this, we can identify that major scales have the following tonal distance formula:

**Tone Tone Semitone Tone Tone Tone Semitone**

What that means is that the distance between the **first note** and the **second note** is **one tone**, the difference between the **second note** and **third note** is **one tone** and so on.

You can apply this formula on any possible note and obtain a new major scale. Of course, the **key signature** of the scale will change. In a future chapter, we will talk about the **circle of 5ths**, which will give us an easier way of figuring out all the possible scales which can be used in songs.

## 4.2 Minor scales explained

**Minor scales** function in a similar manner to **major scales**. They also have 7 notes, which have to be located at certain tonal distances between one another in order to have a proper minor scale.

Let's take the A minor scale as an example. It consists of the A, B, C, D, E, F, G, and A notes. As a result, the formula for minor scales is the following one:

**Tone Semitone Tone Tone Semitone Tone Tone**

What that means is that the distance between the **first note** and the **second note** is **one tone**, the difference between the **second note** and **third note** is **one semitone** and so on.

# Chapter 5 – Harmonic and melodic minor scales

## 5.1 Harmonic minor scales

In the previous chapters, we have discussed minor scales. The minor scales we discussed are also known as **natural minor scales**. However, there are two variations of these scales, which we will talk about today.

The first variation is called the **harmonic minor scale**. This variation is obtained by **raising** the **7th note** of the **natural minor scale** by **one semitone**.

For example, the **harmonic A minor scale** will consist of the A, B, C, D, E, F, G♯, and A notes. Here is how the scale looks like:

## 5.2 Melodic minor scales

A **melodic minor scale** is also obtained by altering the natural minor scale. This time around though, we raise **both** the **6th** and **7th** notes of the said natural minor scale. For example, the **melodic A minor scale** will consist of the A, B, C, D, E, F♯, G♯, and A notes. Here's how it looks like:

# Chapter 6 – Modal scales

**Modal scales** are something that may seem weird at first, but in the end, they are pretty easy to understand.

Let's consider the C major scale. As you know, it consists of the C, D, E, F, G, A, B and C notes. And since there are 7 different notes in a scale, you can actually form a different scale with each and every one of them.

What I mean by that is the following. Let's play all the notes from the C major scale, but instead of starting with C, let's start with D. The resulting scale will contain the following notes: D, E, F, G, A, B, C, and D. As you can see, the formula for this scale is different than the formula for either a major scale or a minor scale.

What we have here is an example of a **modal scale**. More precisely, it's an example of a **Dorian** scale, **D Dorian** to be exact.

And that is exactly what modal scales are. They are scales obtained by playing the notes of a major scale, starting on each of the 7 different notes of the said major scale.

Since there are 7 different notes in a scale, you can have 7 different modal scales, which have the following names:

- **Ionian scale** – this is basically the major scale, which is obtained by playing the notes from the major scale starting on the root note; for example, **C major** can also be referred to as **C Ionian**

- **Dorian scale** – this one is obtained by playing all the notes from the major scale, starting on the **second note**; in the case of C major, its associated Dorian modal scale would be **D Dorian**
- **Phrygian scale** – this one is obtained by playing the notes from the major scale starting on the **third note**; in the case of C major, its associated Phrygian scale would be **E Phrygian**
- **Lydian scale** – obtained by playing the notes of the major scale starting on the **fourth note**; in the case of C major, its associated Lydian scale is **F Lydian**
- **Mixolydian scale** – obtained by playing the notes of the major scale starting on the **fifth note**; in case of C major, its associated Lydian scale is **G Mixolydian**
- **Aeolian scale** – obtained by playing the notes of the major scale starting on the **sixth note**; this is basically the minor relative scale and in the case of C major, that translates to **A Aeolian** or **A minor**
- **Locrian scale** – formed on the **seventh note** of the major scale; for C major, its associated Locrian scale is **B Locrian**

Aside from this method, there is another one in which you can figure out a certain modal scale. There are some formulas with accidentals that you can apply to the **major scale** that will transform it into one of these modal scales. And while the Ionian scale formula is basically…well, you just have to play the major scale…for other scales, some accidentals need to be applied to some of the notes.

Let's check them out, one by one. The **Dorian scale** formula looks like this:

$$1 \ 2 \ \flat3 \ 4 \ 5 \ 6 \ \flat7$$

What that formula above means is that, in order to obtain a **D Dorian scale**, you need to **flatten** the **3rd** and **7th notes** of the **D major scale**.

The **Phrygian scale** formula is the following:

$$1 \ \flat2 \ \flat3 \ 4 \ 5 \ \flat6 \ \flat7$$

This time around, you have to flatten the 2nd, 3rd, 6th, and 7th notes of the major scale.

The **Lydian scale** formula is a bit easier:

$$1 \ 2 \ 3 \ \sharp4 \ 5 \ 6 \ 7$$

As you can see, you need to **sharpen** the fourth note of the major scale in order to obtain the Lydian version of it.

The **Mixolydian scale** formula is also fairly easy:

$$1 \ 2 \ 3 \ 4 \ 5 \ 6 \ \flat7$$

As you can see, you need to flatten the 7th note and presto, it is done.

The **Aeolian scale** formula is the following one:

$$1 \ 2 \ \flat3 \ 4 \ 5 \ \flat6 \ \flat7$$

You'll have to flatten the 3rd, 6th and 7th notes for this one.

And finally, the **Locrian** scale has the following formula:

$$1 \; \flat 2 \; \flat 3 \; 4 \; \flat 5 \; \flat 6 \; \flat 7$$

# Chapter 7 – Pentatonic scales

## 7.1 Major pentatonic scales

**Major pentatonic scales**, much like their minor counterparts, are scales that contain **five notes**. Pentatonic scales are used by guitarists during their solos, especially in rock genres.

And as you're about to see, major and minor pentatonic scales are fairly similar in shape.

In order to obtain a major pentatonic scale, you need to play the **first**, **second**, **third**, **fifth** and **sixth** notes of the **major scale**.

For example, the **C major pentatonic scale** will consist of the C, D, E, G, and A notes.

There are 5 different shapes for this scale on a guitar. Let's start with the one known as the G-form or the G box:

### C Major Pentatonic

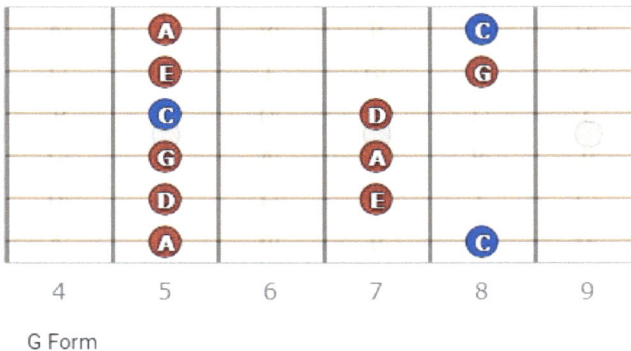

G Form

It's called the G form because if you look closely, it's based on the G shape of the C chord, which looks like this:

```
E | --8-- |
B | --5-- |
G | --5-- |
D | --5-- |
A | --7-- |
E | --8-- |
```

Let's move on to the E-form box:

## C Major Pentatonic

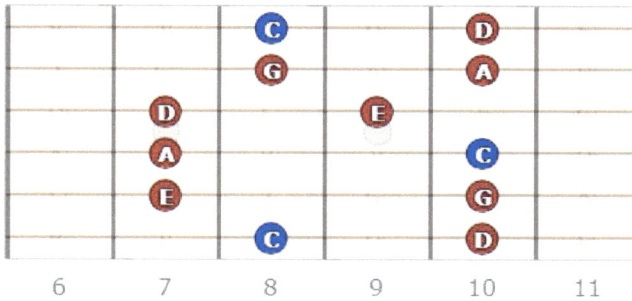

E Form

Next up is the D form:

**C Major Pentatonic**

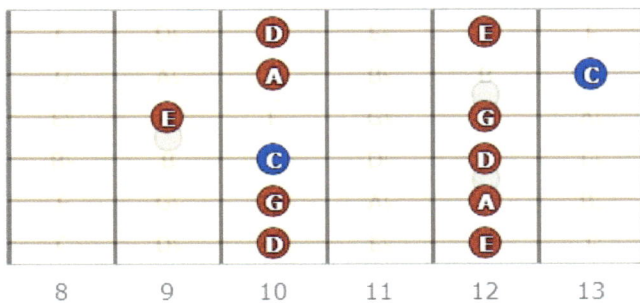

D Form

Next up, the C form:

**C Major Pentatonic**

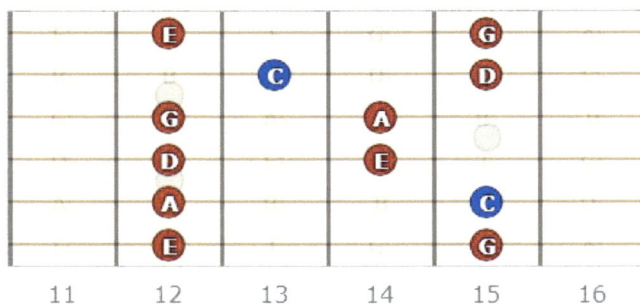

C Form

34

And finally, the A form:

**C Major Pentatonic**

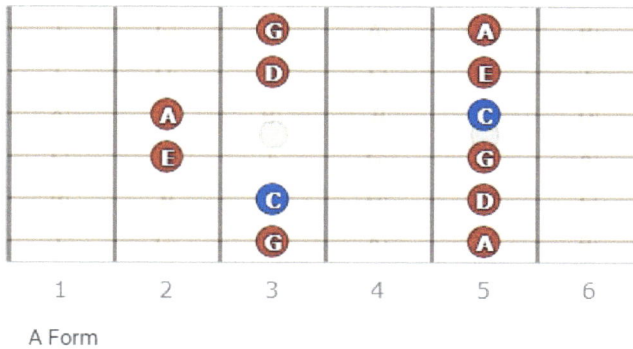

A Form

## 7.2 Minor pentatonic scales

**Minor pentatonic scales** function in a similar manner. Only instead of looking at the major scale, we look at the minor one.

In order to obtain a minor scale, we need to play the **first**, **third**, **fourth**, **fifth** and **seventh notes** of the **minor scale**.

For example, the **A minor pentatonic scale** will consist of the A, C, D, E and G notes. As you can see, the notes are the same ones from the C major pentatonic scale, but in a different order.

Consequently, the shapes in which you can play the A minor pentatonic scale are **the same** as the ones for the C major pentatonic scale.

The only difference is what you consider the root note. Here is what I am referring to, by using the A form. For minor pentatonic though, that form is actually the **G form**:

## A Minor Pentatonic

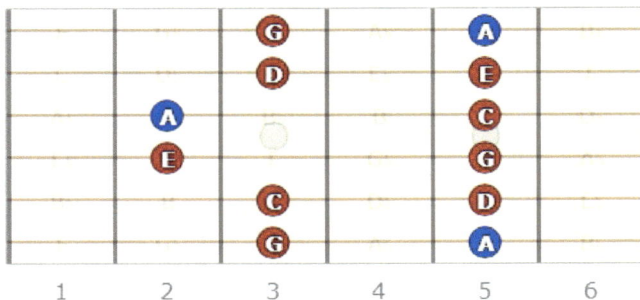

G Form

As you can see, the form is identical, the only difference being what we consider the root note. The same goes for all the forms above. The G form changes its name to the **E form** for minor pentatonic scales:

## A Minor Pentatonic

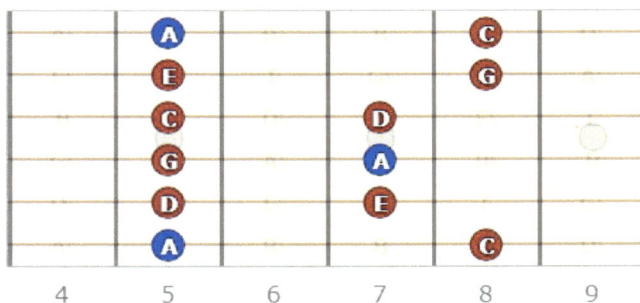

E Form

The E form from above becomes the **D form** now:

## A Minor Pentatonic

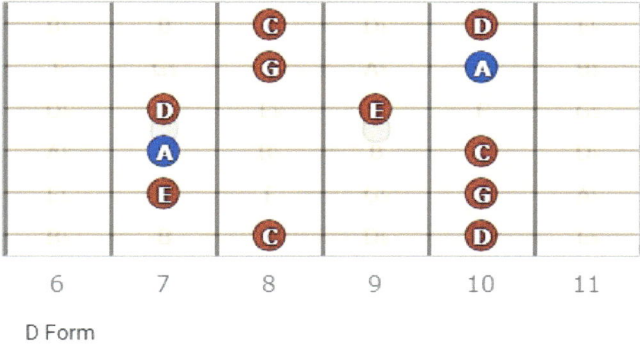

D Form

The D form from above becomes the **C form**:

## A Minor Pentatonic

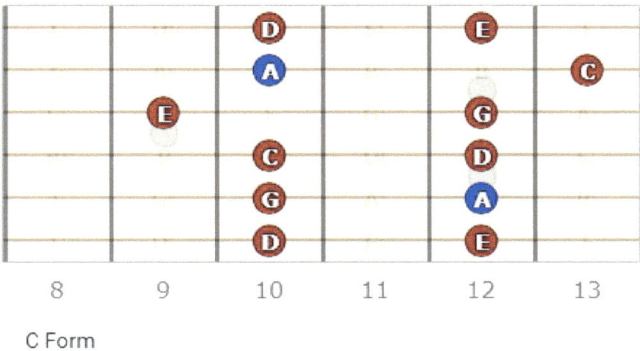

C Form

Finally, the C form from above now becomes the **A form**:

## A Minor Pentatonic

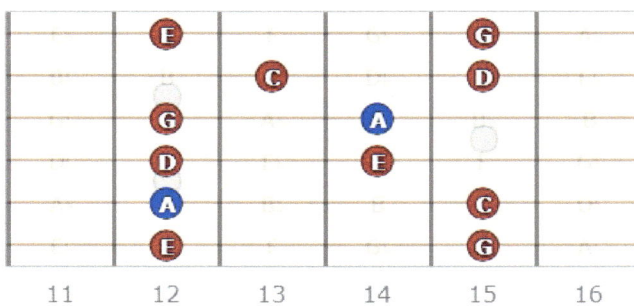

A Form

# Chapter 8 – Chromatic scales

Chromatic scales are quite possibly the easiest of scales to understand. In order to obtain a chromatic scale, you have to play every note located inside an octave.

For example, the C chromatic scale consists of the C, C♯, D, D♯, E, F, G, G♯, A, A♯, B and C notes. Here's how it looks like:

Chromatic scales are neither major nor minor. As for their usage, they aren't used as a whole scale to write a song. Rather, when composing, people tend to use **chromatic tones**, which are notes located outside of the scale the song is written in.

# Chapter 9 – Harmonic minor scale modes

Much like how each major scale has its modal scales, each minor scale can also have different modes. And while the ones for the natural minor scale are the same ones as the ones for its relative major scale, just in a different order, when it comes to harmonic minor scales and melodic minor scales, things are a bit different. The modes have different formulas and consequently will have different names.

What is the same though is the number of modes a harmonic minor scale can have, which is 7. The first one is basically the **harmonic minor scale** itself. And the formula which is based on the major scale is the following:

$$1 \ 2 \ \flat3 \ 4 \ 5 \ \flat6 \ 7$$

Similar to how we built modal scales in the previous chapter, what this translates to is the major scale, but with a flatted **third** and **sixth** notes. For example, the **C major scale** is C D E F G A B while the **C minor harmonic scale** is C D E♭ F G A♭ B.

The next mode is called the **Locrian 13** or **Locrian 6** and has the following formula:

$$1 \ \flat2 \ \flat3 \ 4 \ \flat5 \ 6 \ \flat7$$

Next in line is the **Ionian ♯5,** which has a much simpler formula:

$$1\ 2\ 3\ 4\ ♯5\ 6\ 7$$

The fourth harmonic modal scale is the **Dorian ♯11 (or Dorian ♯4)**, which is basically a Dorian scale, but with a sharpened 4th note:

$$1\ 2\ ♭3\ ♯4\ 5\ 6\ ♭7$$

Next in line is the **Phrygian dominant:**

$$1\ ♭2\ 3\ 4\ 5\ ♭6\ ♭7$$

The penultimate one is the **Lydian ♯2**, which is basically a **Lydian** scale, but with a sharpened 2nd note:

$$1\ ♯2\ 3\ ♯4\ 5\ 6\ 7$$

And I know what you're thinking. Easy enough, just a bunch of flats and sharps here and there. Therefore, I give you the final one, which is called the **Super Locrian ♭♭7:**

$$1\ ♭2\ ♭3\ ♭4\ ♭5\ ♭6\ ♭♭7$$

And yeah, that's actually a double flatted note at the end there.

The funny thing about these modes is that I never really used them all that much, but it seems that they offer quite the possibility in terms of cool sounds. Some examples of how they can be used include but are not limited to:

- **harmonic minor scale** – can be played over minMaj7 chords, or chords like m6, m7, m9, m11, m6/9
- **Locrian 6** – anywhere you play the Locrian mode, generally over half-diminished chords
- **Ionian ♯5** – usually played over **maj7♯5** chords
- **Dorian ♯11** – can be used as an alternative to the Dorian scale and is usually played over minor chords
- **Phrygian dominant** – you can play it for dominant chords to add a bit of Jazz vibe to your songs
- **Lydian ♯2** – usually played over major 7th chords and can act as a substitute to the Lydian scale
- **Super Locrian ♭♭7** – a rarely used scale, but it can be used to great over diminished 7th chords

# Chapter 10 – Melodic minor scale modes

Much like the previous chapter where we learned that harmonic minor scales have modes, so do melodic minor scales have modes. There are still 7 since there are 7 notes. And we are going to talk about each of them here. We are going to look at the formulas for each scale and as usual, the formulas will be based on the major scale.

The first one is basically the **melodic minor scale**, which you may also find under the name of **Jazz Melodic Minor,** which has the following formula:

## 1 2 ♭3 4 5 6 7

Next up is the **Dorian ♭2** scale, which is formed on the second note of the melodic minor scale, and has the following formula:

## 1 ♭2 ♭3 4 5 6 ♭7

Let's move on to the **Lydian augmented** scale, which is formed on the third note of the melodic minor scale, and has the following formula:

## 1 2 3 #4 #5 6 7

The next scale is the **Lydian dominant** scale, which is formed on the **fourth note** of the melodic minor scale and has the following formula:

$$1\ 2\ 3\ \#4\ 5\ 6\ \flat7$$

The fifth one is the **Mixolydian ♭6** scale, which is formed on the 5th note of the melodic minor scale and has the following formula:

$$1\ 2\ 3\ 4\ 5\ \flat6\ \flat7$$

The sixth scale is the **half-diminished** scale, which is formed on the sixth note of the melodic minor scale and has the following formula:

$$1\ 2\ \flat3\ 4\ \flat5\ \flat6\ \flat7$$

Finally, the seventh scale is the **altered scale**, which is formed on the 7th note of the scale and has the following formula:

$$1\ \flat2\ \flat3\ \flat4\ \flat5\ \flat6\ \flat7$$

Here are some pointers on how to use these scales:

- **melodic minor scale**: use over minor chords, min/maj7 chords
- **Dorian ♭2 scale**: can be used ♭9sus4 chords
- **Lydian augmented scale (aka Lydian #5)**: can be used over maj7#5 chords
- **Lydian dominant scale** (aka **Lydian ♭7**): can be used over dominant7(#11) chords
- **Mixolydian ♭6 scale**: can be used over dominant 7(♭13) chords
- **half-diminished scale**: can be used over m7(♭5) chords
- **altered scale**: rarely used, but can be used over dominant chords to some extent

# Chapter 11 – Diminished scales

The **diminished scale** is a very interesting one, mostly because it is a **symmetrical scale**. The formula for it is the following one:

# T S T S T S T

Basically, the difference between the first and second notes is a tone, the difference between the second and third notes is a semitone and so on.

Let's take a look at the **C diminished scale**. It consists of the C, D, E♭, F, G♭, A♭, A and B notes. Here's how it looks like:

The diminished scale can be used in both guitar and piano songs and it can be played over a diminished chord or over a dominant chord.

As you can see, the diminished scale has **8 different notes** rather than 7. Such scales are also known as **octatonic scales**.

# Chapter 12 – Oriental and exotic scales

## 12.1 Oriental scales

The **oriental scale**, which has its origins in China, can be built with the following formula:

**Semitone-Tone and a Semitone-Semitone-Semitone-Tone and a Semitone-Semitone-Tone**

As you can see, it's a scale with larger intervals than the ones we are used to working with.

Let's take a look at a **C oriental scale**. It consists of the C, Db, E, F, Gb, A, Bb, and C notes.

Here's the scale on a music sheet:

## 12.2 Exotic scales

Exotic scales are a group of scales that are based on certain countries or cultures and they can be found under different names.

A comprehensive list of exotic scales can be found here: https://www.pianoscales.org/exotic.html .

# Chapter 13 – Blues scales

## 13.1 Major blues scales

**Blues scales** are very common in guitar songs. There are many versions for them, but the most commonly used blues scales are the ones based on pentatonic scales.

In order to create such a blues scale, you simply need to add a **chromatic tone** to the pentatonic scale.

As you remember, the major pentatonic scale is obtained by playing the first, second, third, fifth and sixth notes of a major scale. And in order to obtain a major blues scale, we need to add a **flatted third note** to this scale.

As a result. the notes of the major blues scale are:

$$1 \ 2 \ \flat3 \ 3 \ 5 \ 6$$

Those are the notes of the major scale which are played as part of the major blues scale. For example, a C major blues scale will consist of the C, D, E♭, E, G, and A notes.

Here are some examples of how you can play the major blues scale, based on major pentatonic scales.

First up, the **A form**:

**C major blues**

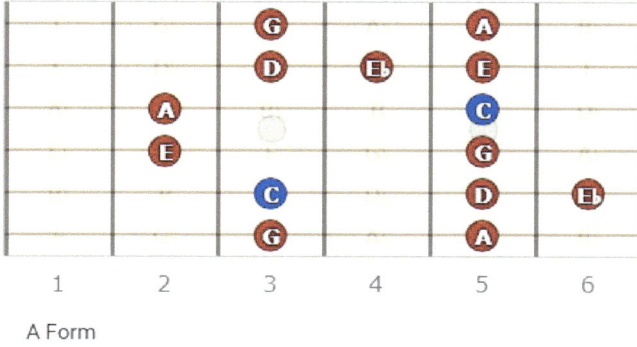

A Form

Next up, the **G form**:

**C major blues**

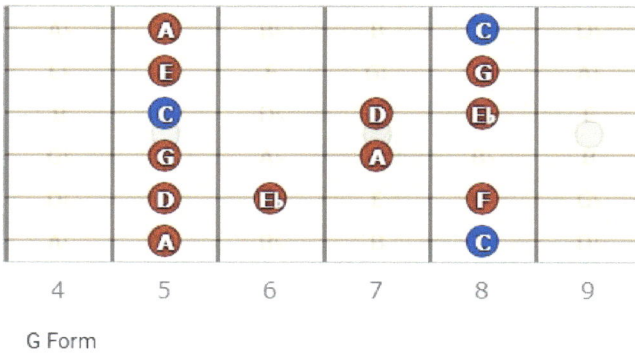

G Form

Next in line is the **E form**:

**C major blues**

E Form

Let's take a look at the **D form** now:

**C major blues**

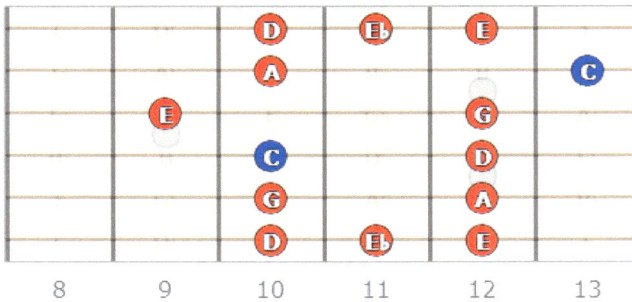

D Form

Finally, let's take a look at the **C form**:

**C major blues**

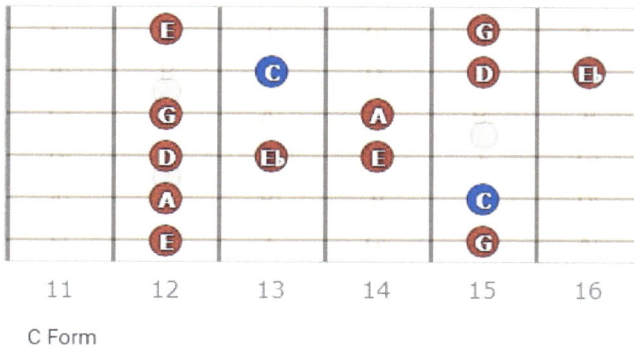

C Form

## 13.2 Minor blues scales

**Minor blues scales** function in a similar manner. The only difference is that you will be adding a **flatted fifth note**. As a result, the formula for them is the following:

$$1\ 3\ 4\ b5\ 5\ 7$$

An example of a minor blues scale would be A minor blues, which consists of the A, C, D, Eb, E and G notes.

Here are some examples of how to play this scale. Let's start with the **G form**:

### A minor blues

G Form

Next up, the **E form**:

### A minor blues

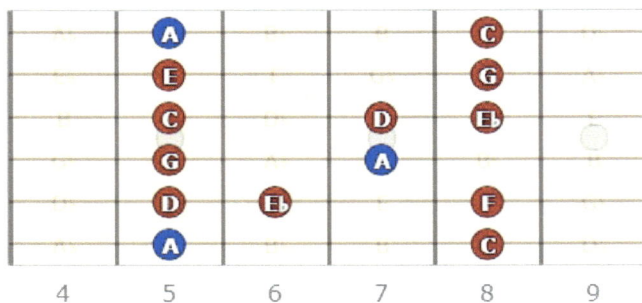

E Form

Next in line, the **D form**:

## A minor blues

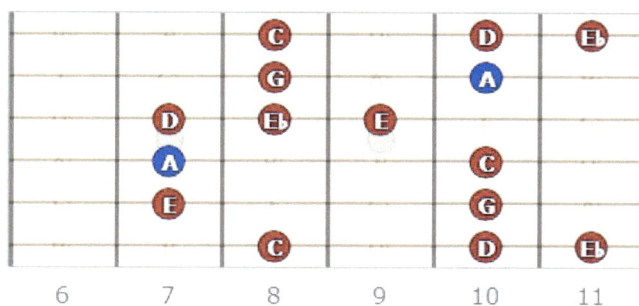

D Form

Another form is the **C form**:

## A minor blues

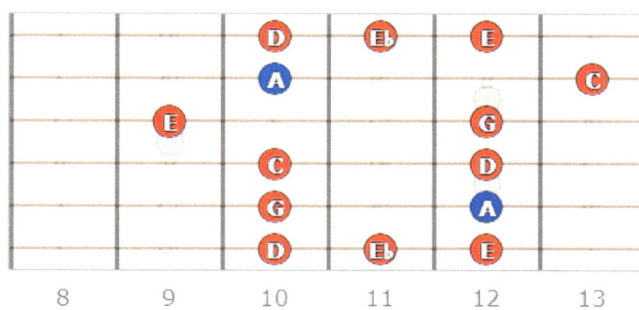

C Form

And finally, the **A form**:

## A minor blues

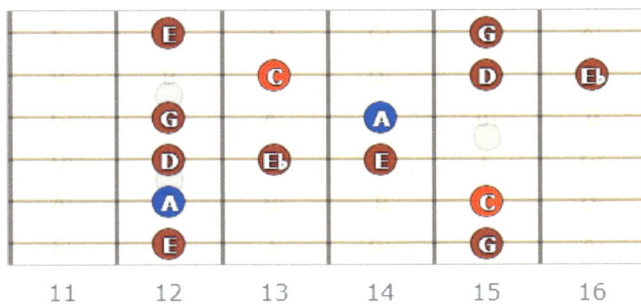

A Form

# Chapter 14 – Conclusion

And another book has reached its conclusion. This one, dedicated to scales, has taken us through all the things needed to understand what scales are and how you can build them.

And with another conclusion, comes a time where I thank you for bearing with me throughout these chapters.

So, what now you ask? Well, feel free to check out other music-related courses you can find around here. Until next time, happy studying.

# References

Pentatonic and blues scales images made with Guitar Scientist:

https://www.editor.guitarscientist.com/new

www.ingramcontent.com/pod-product-compliance
Lightning Source LLC
Chambersburg PA
CBHW041758040426
42447CB00001B/1